For anyone who is struggling—
We see you.
We love you.
Life will get better.
One day at a time.

Have you ever felt dizzy from your **MIND** spinning fast?

Like you're running a race but always coming in last?

Have you ever felt nervous, angry,
or stuck in a funk?

Like no matter

what you do,

you've lost

all your spunk?

If you want to feel good

but are stuck in a bad mood...

Gratitude is a way of saying THANKS
for everything in your life.

It reminds us to BREATHE
in moments of strife.

Even if the world feels scary you can find...

...ways to give thanks
and ways to be KIND.

So here's how you do it, it's simple, you'll see.
In no time at all, CONT NTMEN will come to be!

Start with your B DY, give thanks for all parts.
Your eyes and your ears and your brain—you're so smart!

If you're having trouble,
go to a **CALM**, cozy place.

Then take a deep breath
and sit in that space!

Rest your eyes
and think of things that make you **FEEL JOY**.
Like time with someone special
or your favorite toy.

Maybe it's going to the beach
or playing basketball,

Or that friend who's always
there to **HELP** when you fall.

If something feels happy
and makes your HEART SING,

Carve out time to give thanks to that
person, place, or thing!

Notice all the people in your life who help you GROW.

They send you LOVE each day, setting your heart aglow.

Say "**THANK YOU**" for your warm house
with food on the table,
And for technology and books—from nonfiction to fable.

Give thanks for time with your family
and for GOOD HEALTH.
Gratitude helps us feel good,
it's the ultimate wealth.

Gratitude can change the gray matter of your brain.
It helps you feel good and **RELEASES PAIN**.

It's not the clothes you wear, the house you live in,
or who you know.
Expressing gratitude creates HAPPIER PEOPLE,
science and data show.

Gratitude helps us let go of anger
and **SLEEP BETTER** at night.

It's great to practice if you've had a bad day
or got into a fight.

So whether the day feels
good or terribly blue—

Remember that gratitude is
ALWAYS THERE for you.

Start and end each day
by **CHOOSING**
a positive attitude.

Take the time to express

GRATITUDE!

It's important to note that gratitude can be challenging for us to practice if we're not accustomed to it, especially if you're an adult! Be patient. Keep it simple. Be kind to yourself as you learn and grow!

Ask your child/student questions AFTER reading to check for and reinforce understanding.

Why do we practice gratitude?
To give thanks.

Why is gratitude important?
It makes us happier people! Gratitude helps us focus on the good. It also helps us be better (more empathetic) humans, improves sleep and boosts our self-esteem (how we feel about ourselves).

What is a silver lining?
A silver lining is something positive that comes from a negative experience.

What can you do if you're having trouble thinking of what you're grateful for?
Begin with your body—your eyes and your ears and your brain—you're so smart!

Think of a situation where it would be helpful to practice gratitude.
If there's a storm outside and you're frustrated or afraid, remind yourself of the plants that the rain is feeding and the rainbow that follows!

FIND THE SILVER LINING

Directions: A silver lining is finding something positive in a negative experience. Match each negative experience to the silver lining below!

Negative Experience:

Thunderstorm

Rain

Falling down while playing basketball

Spilling cereal on the kitchen floor

Silver Lining:

Friend helps you up

Dog happily cleans up

Cuddling with your pet

Feeding flowers

Activity 2

WHAT ARE YOU GRATEFUL FOR?

Write in the circles or draw a picture!

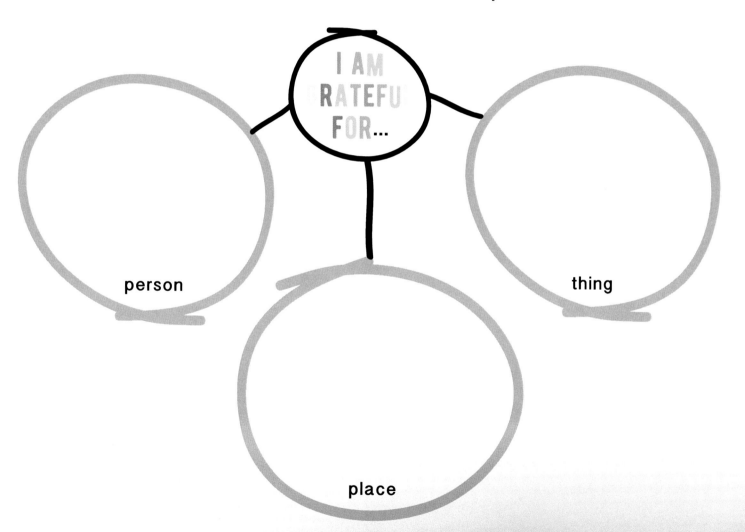

person

I AM GRATEFUL FOR...

thing

place

GLOSSARY

attitude: a way of feeling or acting toward a person, thing or situation.

calm: feeling free; the absence of strong emotions.

contentment: being happy and satisfied.

fable: a made-up story, typically with animals as the main characters.

funk: a bad mood.

gray matter: the brain's outer layer that helps us understand language and information (also called the cerebral cortex).

gratitude: being thankful.

nonfiction: writing based on real facts, real events and real people.

spunk: courage, spirit.

strife: a conflict or something that is difficult.

wealth: having a lot of money or possessions.

WE A
GIVE YO R B AIN A BA H B OKS
ARE G ATEFUL OR...

...ALL OF OUR AMAZING

READERS LIKE YOU!

Made in the USA
Middletown, DE
11 September 2022

73433764R00027